D1796058

1 MONTH OF
FREE
READING

at

www.ForgottenBooks.com

By purchasing this book you are eligible for one month membership to ForgottenBooks.com, giving you unlimited access to our entire collection of over 1,000,000 titles via our web site and mobile apps.

To claim your free month visit:

www.forgottenbooks.com/free130902

* Offer is valid for 45 days from date of purchase. Terms and conditions apply.

ISBN 978-0-483-81818-7
PIBN 10130902

This book is a reproduction of an important historical work. Forgotten Books uses
state-of-the-art technology to digitally reconstruct the work, preserving the original format
whilst repairing imperfections present in the aged copy. In rare cases, an imperfection in
the original, such as a blemish or missing page, may be replicated in our edition. We do,
however, repair the vast majority of imperfections successfully; any imperfections that
remain are intentionally left to preserve the state of such historical works.

Forgotten Books is a registered trademark of FB &c Ltd.
Copyright © 2018 FB &c Ltd.
FB &c Ltd, Dalton House, 60 Windsor Avenue, London, SW19 2RR.
Company number 08720141. Registered in England and Wales.

For support please visit www.forgottenbooks.com

REPORTS

PRESENTED TO THE

WESTERN-CONFERENCE

OF

UNITARIAN CHURCHES,

HELD AT

LOUISVILLE, MAY, 1854.

PRINTED BY ORDER OF THE CONFERENCE.

LOUISVILLE:

HULL AND BROTHER.

M D CCC LIV.

III. 8518

C 8160.7

Harvard College Library

From the Library of

Rev. A. P. Peabody.

18 Oct. 1893.

EXTRACT FROM MINUTES.

SATURDAY, 13 May, 1854.

Upon motion of Rev. W. G. Eliot,—

RESOLVED—That we have heard with much profit the Report of Judge Pirtle, and that it be referred to the Executive Committee to be printed.

RESOLVED—However, that under our organization as the Conference of Western Unitarian Churches, we have no right to adopt any statement of belief as authoritative, or as a declaration of Unitarian Faith, other than the New Testament itself, which is the divinely authorized rule both of faith and practice.

RESOLVED—That we earnestly recommend to the churches and societies here represented by us, to adhere more and more closely to the direct instructions of our Lord Jesus Christ; that we may become living branches of the true vine, and bring forth the Christian fruit of good works to the glory of God.

Upon motion, N. P. Sprague, Esq.—

RESOLVED—That the above Resolutions be published as a preface to the Report.

(Signed)   W. D. HALEY,
SECRETARY OF CONFERENCE.

Ann...

Jesus ... Christ
& Unitarianism ...

REPORT ON

UNITARIAN VIEWS OF CHRIST,

PRESENTED BY

CHANCELLOR PIRTLE.

RESOLUTION.

AT the Conference held at St. Louis last May, the following Preamble and Resolutions were introduced and referred to a Committee :—

"As there is misunderstanding of the views of Unitarian Christians on important subjects, it is deemed proper to make some declaration in reference thereto.

"RESOLVED—That we regard Jesus Christ not as a mere inspired man, but as the Son of God; the messenger of the Father to men, miraculously sent; the mediator between God and man; the redeemer of the world: That we regard the miracles of the New Testament as facts, on which the gospel is based."

That Committee have had the same under consideration, and now respectfully present this as their Report.

REPORT.

WE think there is much misunderstanding of what is believed, and what is not believed, by Unitarian Christians; and that it is proper at this time to make a short statement of our faith, with regard to some matters about which it is probable we are most misunderstood and misrepresented. It is due to the cause of the truth we hold, that we shall not be deemed to hold what is opposed to this truth. If we believe the miracles of the New Testament, and hold them to be the historical foundation of the Gospel, it is not proper that we allow ourselves to be represented to any men as disbelieving, or holding other views. We who believe in Christ should profess Christ; and it is a part of this duty to our Saviour, not to allow ourselves to be placed with any who do not honor his name.

We know there have been sincere and pious persons who have held that the Saviour's existence commenced on earth, but who also have held to his divine authority—as one speaking from God—in whom was the manifestation of God to men. And there are yet some who hold such a view, whose christian walk, whose pious lives, are not less exemplary than the lives of those who hold otherwise. None but God has dominion over their faith.

Should it be said by any, that it is not important whether we believe that Jesus was a mere inspired man, or above all mankind—that the fullness and authority of the Heavenly Father could be made to dwell in a man, as well as in one surpassing all angels and archangels; to such we say, all Divine Truth is important; and whatsoever has been revealed concerning the character of the Heavenly Messenger, can not but be worthy of our very highest attention and veneration.

If it had pleased the Almighty, our salvation

could have been wrought out by a man. This we cannot deny, unless we suppose a limitation to the infinite power of the Deity. But what in His wisdom, has been done, is our inquiry, not what might have been done.

We profess to rely on the Holy Scriptures as our guide in all matters of Christian Faith. We reject the authority of man, and turn with reverence and trust to what is taught by God. We offer no creed to our fellow men — we cannot make any. We reject the creeds made by other men, because we have the same Revelation which they had, and have reason to believe, as a matter of history, that what was written down by them to bind after generations, was not free from outward, temporary influence, and was not the offspring of more intelligence, and more enlightened piety than belong to succeeding ages. We do not withhold a suitable deference for the opinions of our fellow men in this day, or in former days. Regard for the belief of men, as some evidence of truth, is natural and proper; but it is often delusive, and a blind submission to it takes away all independent thought, and fixes a false basis of religious faith. *The opinion of millions cannot supersede the Scriptures.* We dare not yield them an instant, to the creed of *succeeding millions.* A creed* that was a part of the liturgy of the whole christian world for centuries,—though not admitted by any council as far as we know—and which is still contained in the liturgies of the majority of all Christians, was rejected by the general convention of the Protestant Episcopal Church held at Wilmington in October, 1786, and is rejected by all Protestant Christians in America. Here is a memorable instance where the authority of ages, and of generations that filled the world, was made to give way to thought, to investigation, to progress.

I. As the subject of the trinity is necessarily

* Called the Athanasian Creed.

connected with what we hold in regard to the person of Christ, it is deemed proper to offer a few thoughts on that doctrine, without pretending to discuss the subject at large.

We cordially believe in the Father, Son, and Holy Spirit, and in all that the Scriptures teach in regard to them. But while we thus believe, we reject the doctrine of a Deity in three persons, because it is not revealed in the Scriptures. God is there, as He is in Nature, declared to be one. There is no such word as trinity in the Bible; and there is no such declaration there, as that there are three persons and one God. To be a person, in the sense in which the word is now used, is to have a separate or independent consciousness; the word absolutely implies this.* The Great Creator has so formed the minds of all men, that *number*, and the distinction of one thing, or number, *from another*

* This is from the Latin word PERSONA, which as often meant character or representation, as the individual man or being. In that sense it was probably used by such of the earlier Christians as professed to be Trinitarians; and in such a sense as that, we do not object to the doctrine of the Trinity.

thing, or number, cannot be removed by any effort. THIS IS GOD'S LAW OF OUR MINDS. We can conceive of the truth of hundreds of things that are mysterious to us; and we can believe things that we cannot understand. All around is filled with mystery. All life is mystery. But there is a great difference between a mystery, or something we do not understand, and a *contradiction*, or an absurdity. We cannot *believe* a contradiction; we cannot believe an absurdity. We may *assent* to it, and think we believe it, because it is written down for us by what we have been taught to regard as holy authority; but we do not. We might as well take the thought of number, the conception of identity and of difference from the human mind, as to believe that three persons (which implies, as the word means now, three beings, as far as distinct consciousness is concerned) can be one person, and that one person can be three persons. God was proclaimed as one person from Sinai — was held to be one person by those among whom our Lord walked in this world; was prayed to as such by those who worshiped where he taught his doctrine—in the Temple and in the Synagogue,—and was worshiped as one person by our Lord in the presence of his disciples and of the people: "*I thank thee, O Father, Lord of heaven and earth.*" And to this day, the descendants of those to whom the true God was revealed, hold Him to be one. Had Jesus, whose business it was to teach and to preach daily in the Synagogues and in the Temple, his peculiar doctrine, taught that the God of Abraham existed in three persons, it would surely have been mentioned by the Evangelists; for nothing could have so struck these authors; nothing could have been so as-tonishing to the Jews; and nothing could have produced so great a commotion in their Syna-gogues. But instead of that, we hear him say, quoting from their law, "Hear, O Israel, the Lord our God is one Lord." Mark xii : 29.

St. Paul, in his travels for the propagation of

the new religion, went continually into the Jewish Synagogues, in different parts of the world, to preach the Gospel. He was thrust out sometimes; but not for declaring this doctrine. If he had preached that the God of the Hebrews was in three persons, and, of course, that Jesus was one, can it be possible that he would not have always been thrust out, or that there should be no record that he ever was, for such cause?

Every one who reads the Scriptures, must feel, must acknowledge, that there is a superiority given to the Father. . This appears continually; it cannot be denied. Is there a man in the world who has read the New Testament that can deny this? The very idea that there is a Son sent and a Holy Spirit given, plainly speaks it. This, then, is an end of the proposition of the creeds — nothing can be superior to, and yet be the same with, the inferior. That would be, not a mystery, but a contradiction. In St. Peter's sermon, (Acts ii.)

when the Gospel was first preached after the resurrection, attended by the miraculous gift of tongues, so that the people of the nations might understand it, and when three thousand were converted and baptized, there is no mention of such a subject; and it is impossible that those who heard him, could from his recorded language, have had any notion of such a doctrine as that set forth in the creeds. Had it been a part of the Christian faith, we should have expected it here. So in the tenth chapter of Acts, when Peter preached to the neighbors of Cornelius — the first preaching to the Gentiles separately — there is nothing said which could give the least intimation to those people, who were also converted and baptized, that there was such a doctrine belonging to the Gospel of Christ.

It may be said that the doctrine of the trinity was too abstruse to be preached by Peter on these occasions — that the people could not have understood him; that it might have hindered the acceptance of the Gospel. If this were true, it would show plainly that it cannot be an essential article of faith; for "To the poor the Gospel is preached;" "the common people heard him gladly;" and the religion of Christ does especially bring peace and joy to the humble and the untaught and unintellectual.

We cannot consent to the doctrine of the trinity as stated in the creeds, because it cannot be supported without the admission as a fact, that *to the Eternal and* INFINITE GOD, *the Maker of all Worlds and Systems of Worlds, there is annexed, or united, a* HUMAN BODY AND SOUL; for, if Jesus was not a man, in body and soul, as well as the Infinite Jehovah, then his prayers to the Father, and his often repeated declarations of his inferiority and separate existence, leave *no place* for such a doctrine. It must have been humanity only that prayed and spoke, as the creeds would have it, or the argument is over. These two natures, one of weakness, and perishing in pain and death, and the other the Sublime Majesty and Beatitude of God, must have been united in one person, in one consciousness — impossible as it is to imagine it — or the Saviour was in his person — his existence — not the Self-existent Being of Eternity.

If the doctrine of the trinity, as written in the creeds of men, had been an essential faith of the Gospel, we think it must have been declared by our Lord himself, and by his Apostles, in plain language; and not left to be eked out by ingenious polemics — a baffling enigma. If this had been a *fact* of the Gospel of Christ, we cannot believe that our blessed Lord (we speak with reverence) would have left it in such perplexing obscurity.

The history of Christianity shows beyond doubt, that there was no such doctrine in the Church in the ages immediately succeeding the Apostles.

In the venerable formula called the Apostles' Creed, the oldest known — older than the Nicene or the Athanasian,— though no one now pretends it was composed by the Apostles,— there is no mention of a trinity; but the contrary is the plain reading of the instrument. It is decidedly Unitarian.

Indeed, putting all other argument aside, the very thought of Deity excludes the trinity of persons. God is a Self-existent Being. There can be but one self-existent being; for He must in His nature be infinite and undivided; and from Him must all other beings, or persons, or things, proceed.

These are some of the reasons why, although we heartily believe in the Father and the Son and the Holy Spirit, yet we do not hold the doctrine of the trinity as it is stated in the creeds of men. We hold firmly to the strict unity of God. "To us there is but one God the Father, of whom are all things, and we in Him; and one Lord Jesus Christ, by whom are all things and we by Him." 1 Cor. viii: 6.

II. IN the next place, although we do not acknowledge the doctrine of the trinity, yet let us make a short inquiry as to what the Scripture doctrine is in regard to the character of Christ.

The Scriptures call Jesus the *Son of God;* "the only begotten Son which is in the bosom of the Father." It is not possible to conceive of any higher rank of derived being than is implied by these expressions. No language that we could think of, could so powerfully express the Saviour's nearness to God — the divinity of His NATURE. The mystery of His existence we cannot fathom; we can have no conception of its origin in the course of eternity; or of the impartation of the Divine Power. "It pleased *the Father* that in Him should all fulness dwell." According to the Scriptures, the power that He exercised on earth, was the power of God. His acts were the acts of God. It was the Father working by Him. His salvation wrought out for man, was wrought by God, was the salvation of God, properly and wholly, according to the declaration of our Lord himself.

As to his existence before he appeared among men, it seems to us that the sacred writings do show this fact. The whole tenor of Scripture places the Lord Jesus Christ altogether above an inspired man. It would be tedious to quote all the passages which so exalt him. Throw aside all speculations of philosophy, read naturally as you do any other writings, looking for facts stated, and it seems plain to us, any reader will acknowledge that in the body of the New Testament, Christ is presented as no prophet, no angel — no being but one next to God is held forth to men. "Wherefore, when he cometh into the world, he saith, sacrifice and offering thou wouldest not, but a body hast thou prepared me." . . . . "Then said he, Lo, I come to do Thy will, O God." Heb. x: 5, 9. This language expresses that a previous being comes from another place to dwell in a body mad here — a body is prepared; not a soul. The miraculous generation of Jesus, as stated in the Evangelists, indicates that he was not a mere man, but higher than a man; and seems to be the fulfilment of the prophecy quoted from the Psalms by the author of Hebrews.

Our Lord continually represented himself as having been *sent*. "He that believeth on me, believeth not on me, but on Him that sent me." "For I have not spoken of myself, but the Father which sent me, He gave me a commandment, what I should say, and what I should speak." John xii. "Jesus knowing that the Father had given all things into his hands, and that he was come from God and went to God." John xiii. "I came out from God." "I came forth from the Father and am come into the world; again I leave the world and go to the Father." John xvi. In this chapter it is stated by the disciples as a matter of faith, to believe that he came forth from God. Now, every man and every creature does, in one

sense, come forth from God; and if this were
the sense to be understood, there would be no
reason for our Lord's dwelling upon this fact
so continually, or for any belief on the part
of the disciples. But it is a matter of
faith in the disciples of Christ; and in the majestic prayer of the Saviour in the seventeenth
chapter it is again presented in the sublime connection with the glorification of the Son of God.
"And this is life eternal, that they might know
Thee, the only true God and Jesus Christ whom
Thou hast sent. I have glorified Thee on the
earth, I have finished the work which Thou gavest me to do. And now, O Father, glorify Thou
me with Thine own self, with the glory which I
had with Thee before the world was." Refer-
ring to his disciples, the prayer proceeds, " Now
they have known that all things whatsoever
Thou hast given me are of Thee. For I have
given unto them the words which Thou gavest
me; and they have received them, and have
known surely that I came out from Thee, and

they have believed that Thou didst send me.

He is placed above angels in the first chapter of Hebrews; and whether the author means in his quotations from the Psalms to use them only as illustrations of his meaning, or to refer to them as prophecies speaking of Christ, he applies them so as to show that he deems the Saviour the highest of all derived beings.

St. Paul says in Col. i: 15–19, "Who is the image of the invisible God, the first born of every creature. For by Him were all things created that are in heaven, and that are in earth, visible and invisible, whether they be thrones, or dominions, or principalities, or powers: all things were created by Him, and for Him: and He is before all things and by Him all things consist; and He is the head of the body, the Church: who is the beginning, the first born from the dead; that in all things He might have the pre-eminence. For it pleased the Father that in Him should all fulness dwell."

He had power to forgive sins, and he worked miracles, in his own name. He has grace to dispense to his disciples, as so often expressed by St. Paul in his benedictions; and glory for-ever and ever is made the ascription to him by St. Peter, and St. Paul, and Revelation.

Whatever may be the just interpretation of the passage quoted from the Colossians, it is evident that it was meant to express that Christ is, in some sense, next to God in pre-eminence, and that his existence is derived and his power conferred by the "Father," the "Invisible God;" just as when Jesus says in the last chapter of Matthew, "All power is given me in heaven and in earth," it is a strong expression of his pre-eminence, though it is evident from the context that it is a moral power for the protection of his follow-ers and the government of his Church. And it is equally evident that the power he has is "given" by another; and He who is the source of "all power," cannot divest himself so as to be left neutral and helpless in the universe.

When our Lord declared to his disciples that he was inferior to his Father, it was at once the strongest declaration of his superiority to man; for there could have been no possible motive for such a declaration to the disciples, if he were a man such as they — to say that God is greater than a man, affords no instruction.

We, then, as Unitarians, instead of detracting from the elevation of the Saviour, would contemplate his exaltation as a Divine Person beyond the imagination of man to conceive. *" No man knoweth the Son, but the Father."*

III. WE believe then in Christ as possessed of this exalted nature, as being indeed the Son of the living God.

The doctrine of two natures in Christ is nowhere mentioned in the Scriptures; but it was resorted to, to uphold and complete the trinity doctrine of the creeds begun at the Council of Nice. It originated in a semi-barbarous age; and it was established in its present form at a time when strife and persecution, bloodshed, banishment, and death were the agents by which religious opinions were enforced on mankind. The Council of Ephesus, which had this doctrine under consideration, was marked by the beating of a bishop in the church where it was held, so that he died of his wounds. The judgment of this Council not being satisfactory to the Western bishop, a Council was called at Nice in Bithynia to re-consider the subject. That the new emperor and empress might be able to exercise their immediate influence, it was adjourned to Chalcedon, opposite Constantinople, where the control of the imperial authority established the doctrine of the two natures, as we now have it, as there is every reason to believe from the history of that Council.

Its establishment was attended by a sentence of banishment of the bishop of Alexandria, executed by the emperor, and the condemnation of Eutyches, who was not summoned, not present, and not heard. Is such a tribunal a fit authority over the faith of American Christians in 1854?

The doctrine established by this body in the year 451, is thus set forth: "That in Christ *two distinct persons* [*natures*] were united in *one person*, and that without any change, mixture, or confusion." "That he was truly God and truly man." "Never to be divided," says the second article of the Protestant Episcopal Church. "And continueth to be God and man, in two *distinct* natures, and one person forever," says the Westminster Catechism. The natures are in no manner commixed; for that would make a being who would neither be God nor man,—but still they make one person; that is to say, they are united so as to be one, but they are not united! We understand that a person is distinguished by will, mind, consciousness. If there be a nature that has a separate mind, will, motive, consciousness, understanding, it is not the same person with that other which has not this mind, will, consciousness, understanding. But if they are united so as to have one mind, one thought, will, understanding, consciousness, then they are one, identical—this is what we understand by *person*. Now, it is a downright contradiction to say that God's nature can be united to man's nature and become one person; and still, have separate consciousness. They cannot become one person any more than infinite can be made finite. God is eternal, infinite, omnipotent, omniscient, the creator of all things, incapable of suffering, perfectly happy—He holds the universe in His hands—He is the same yesterday, and to-day, and forever; it is but to state an absurdity in the strongest form, to say He was indissolubly united with the nature of man, with imperfect knowledge, weakness, subject to sorrow, to disease and death. But it is not less absurd to say they still retain these opposite qualities and are one person — not even divided, but one at the death of the cross. And we insist on stronger testimony than the votes of councils formed of fallible and sometimes intolerent men, in an unenlightened age, before we can admit that such an impossibility is inculcated as a sound doctrine of the Bible. The nature of things must stand unchanged by the decrees of men. Shall any one say, "All is possible with God," and therefore you say too much when you say it is an impossibility: we say no: God has so ordered that there cannot be any contradiction in His government. He cannot make it light and dark in the same place, or a thing to be and not to be at the same time.

A comparison is sometimes made between the union of our bodies and spirits, and two natures in Christ. But this is merely delusive. There is no analogy. We are composed of soul and body, but we have one nature, one person, one consciousness—our bodies have weight, solidity, length, shape; we know not that our souls have; but there is no *contradiction* in their union; and here is the fallacy in the comparison; here is the entire want of analogy. In the one case there is an assemblage of incompatible qualities; in the other there is no incompatibility, but natural union.

This doctrine of the two natures unquestionably makes two persons; for one does still remain with the limited intellect of man, and subject to weakness, while the other is the omniscient and omnipotent God; if one fills immensity, and is beyond the imagination of the other to conceive; or if one even thinks what the other does not, they are two. The doctrine is just so esteemed by those who hold it; for they say that when Jesus spoke of his inferiority, of his want of knowledge, etc., he spoke in his human nature; that when he suffered pain, it was in his humanity; when he aid, "My soul is exceeding sorrowful, even unto death," he meant his human soul, for God lives in brightness and glory.

But there is another objection to this doctrine, not metaphysical at all, but quite as conclusive. Even to speak of it fills us with awe. The doctrine implicates the explicit sincerity of our Lord. O, how can we allow man to make the Saviour speak in a double sense! When he said, "I can of mine own self do nothing," this doctrine makes him speak with a mental reservation. When he said this, he necessarily meant the "own self" in the way he knew those addressed would understand him; otherwise we make an imputation on his truth; and when he said, "My Father is greater than I," he spoke with a mental reserve; although the pronoun was used that included his whole person, and when if his person included Deity, it could not be true; and further, the truth was too plain for any necessity of inculcation, if he was to be understood to speak in a human nature—and so in the numerous

3

instances when he spoke of his acts not being his own, but of Him that sent him. So in the remarkable declaration of his want of knowledge in the thirteenth chapter of Mark; and when he said, "Why callest thou me good, there is none good but one, that is God." Now, if he had all power; if he was one with the Father, not different; if he was good (in the sense implied) and was God, this language (we speak it with 'reverence) seems to us to make those who heard him misunderstand the truth. He had taught his apostles such truth with regard to his character, as was necessary to salvation—this we may assume. He had taught them that he came out from God, and they professed this belief in such manner as to show that they did believe him to be more than a man;—the true doctrine was believed by them at any rate—and we may suppose he had taught Mary what, concerning him, should be necessary to her salvation—for who was a better disciple than she who was "ear.

liest at his grave,"—yet, with this instruction given them, after his resurrection he says to Mary, "Go to my brethren and say unto them, I ascend unto my Father and your Father, and to my God and your God." Can there be such mental reserve here? Does not this show plainly that he who was born and came into the world to "bear witness to the truth," was the messenger of God, but had not the nature, was not the person, of God.

There is no conduct on the part of the disciples, mentioned in the Gospels, that indicates the astonishment and awe that must have overcome them, if at any time it had been revealed that he was God! Their deportment, all the while shows plainly that they had no thought of any thing so overwhelming; and it appears that their belief in the true character of Jesus, that he came forth from God, was expressed even *after the last supper.* "His disciples said unto him, Lo, now speakest thou plainly, and speakest no proverb. Now are we sure that thou knowest all things, and needest not that any man should ask thee; by this we believe that thou camest forth from God."

But in that passage in Mark xiii: 32, surely it is shown absolutely that our Lord did not mean any reserve. When he said, "But of that day and that hour knoweth no man, no, not the angels which are in heaven, neither the Son, but the Father," he spoke in his whole character, and he included the ranks of existence mentioned in the Bible, man, angel, the Son, the Father. The Son is spoken of here plainly, as more than man or angel, and is as plainly and expressly declared to have less knowledge than the Father. Is there any man in the world that can read this verse and say it does not declare that the Son did *not* know what God *must* know? One explicit declaration in the words of Jesus, made without metaphor, or any figure of speech, must be sufficient to establish any *fact* of the

Gospel; it overturns all inferences from passages hard to be understood; and stands against all that could be said by men in high places, or any places; and whatever may have been said by men in any numbers, or in ages upon ages, must fall before this: "Heaven and earth shall pass away; but my words shall not pass away." Mark xiii: 31.

Our Lord prayed fervently to the Father. Now, if the true God, the Father, was united with the person of Christ, it was the same person praying to the same person; for if two natures made one person, and one nature prayed to the other nature, it is just as contradictory. The consciousness must be separate—there must be two intelligences in the instance of prayer—it must be from one to the other; and then there are two beings, or persons.

The Westminster Catechism says, "it was requisite that the Mediator should be God, that He might sustain and keep the human nature from sinking under the infinite wrath of God and the power of death," etc. St. Luke says, that at the time of his agony, "there appeared an angel unto him from heaven, strengthening him." Surely if he was God he did not need the help of an angel — his humanity if united in one person to ALL POWER, could not have been strengthened by any other. If the Source of Strength was present, we cannot conceive that an inferior should be sent from heaven. The passage is calculated to delude us, if this were so; but it reads very plainly, if Christ was a dependent being. So when Peter struck the servant of the High Priest in defense of Jesus, he said to him, "Thinkest thou that I cannot now pray to my Father and he shall presently give me more than twelve legions of angels?" If he possessed the power of God, and was God, why should he speak of the assistance he might get by prayer to his Father? It certainly was calculated to convey to Peter the impression that he was dependent on God his Father.

In the tenth chapter of John, our Lord says, "I and my Father are one." But in his prayer in the seventeenth chapter, he twice prays that his disciples might be one as he and his Father were one. "That they may be one, even as we are one."

This doctrine is only necessary to support the other creed made by the vote of a council, and not necessary to make an exalted victim for the sacrifice of atonement; for it cannot be contended that any but human nature suffered and died; nor can any man for a moment suppose that the great Author of Life died upon the cross! Yet it was established at the fifth ecumenical council held at Constantinople, that "one of the trinity suffered on the cross"—and this was put into the creed to please the Emperor. How awful, when we pause and think of it, is the presumption of such an assertion! Its absurdity, however, does not surpass the other position that the two natures of God and man were united in one person. The deduction made at Constantinople was but the fair inference from what was fixed as doctrine at Chalcedon. In the Catechism of the Council of Trent, page 46, when speaking of the words in the Apostles' Creed, "dead and buried," it is stated: "It is not, however, our belief that the body of Christ was alone interred: these words propose as the principal object of our belief, that *God was buried;* as according to the rule of the Catholic faith we also say, with the strictest truth, that *God* was born of a virgin, that *God* died; for as the divinity was never separated from his body which was laid in the sepulchre, we truly confess that *God was buried.*" And now in the hymns of our Christian brethren, we read such lines as these:

> God the mighty Maker, died
> For man, the creature's sin;

And

> The risen God forsakes the tomb;

And these—

> The moment a sinner believes,
> And trusts in his crucified God.

With the kindest feelings for our brethren, we cannot suppress our wonder that they should use language expressing sentiments so unjustified by scripture, and so opposing the natural reason that God has given to all men.

We reject these doctrines, because they have been put on Christianity by frail men like ourselves; they obscure religion; they fill the faith of Christians with contradictions, absurdities, and impossibilities; and they are calculated, on this account, to turn many reflecting minds away from the devout study and acceptance of revealed truth. When such minds have been moved by the Spirit of God to look to the precepts of the Gospel, they have found these enigmas covering its simple pages. When we speak thus, using such words as 'absurdities,' we mean no reflection on our brethren who hold these doctrines — we speak only in a philosophical sense. We respect and love them for their piety, their zeal, and their blameless lives.

IV. HAVING thus presented our views in regard to the strict unity of God and the nature of Our Saviour, we will offer a few thoughts respecting the Holy Spirit.

In the Holy Spirit we heartily believe, but not in its distinct, independent personality.

It was not until fifty-six years after the Council of Nice, which established the Deity of Christ, that the personality of the Holy Spirit was decreed. This was done at the Council of Constantinople, A. D. 381; and it was enforced by the Emperor Theodosius by edicts of disfranchisement, confiscation, and exile. The manner in which this doctrine was fixed on the Church should make us withhold all deference to the authority that placed it there. The clergy of that age had scandalously degenerated from Apostolic purity, and this Council was exceedingly turbulent and overbearing. The tyrant emperor had his way. Let us throw aside this decree, and look at the subject with the Bible in our hands.— *Look at it* naturally.

Among the Ancient People with whom the "Oracles of God" were deposited, there was no such thought as that the Spirit so often mentioned, was a person; and there is no expression in the Old Testament that would even seem to intimate such a thing to any reader. In the New Testament we first find the expression Holy Ghost, in our translation. This word ghost was used at the time of this translation, in the same sense in which we use the word spirit; and the word which is translated, means literally, breath or wind in the original, and has no proper meaning of person. What is said of the Spirit has a plain reference to God himself; or the power of God; or the influence or communication of God. Look at the passages in the New Testament where the expression Holy Ghost, or Holy Spirit, is used: In the twelfth chapter of Matthew, and third of Mark, and twelfth of Luke, where they speak of blasphemy against the Holy Ghost, it may mean God, the power of God, or the influence or communication of God; and it is fair to say, that, if there is such a proper person as contended for, it may mean that. And in the appointment of baptism, it may mean the power, or influence, impartation of God's Spirit, or in propriety of language, it might mean, the proper personality spoken of. When Jesus speaks of the Comforter in the fourteenth, fifteenth, and sixteenth chapters of John, the Comforter is called the Holy Ghost, or Spirit, "even the Spirit of Truth; whom the world cannot receive, because it seeth him not, neither knoweth him; but ye know him; *for he dwelleth with you, and shall be in you.*" "But when the Comforter is come, whom I will send unto you from the Father, even the Spirit of Truth which *proceedeth* from the Father, he shall testify of me." Now, evidently, fair reasoning would say that this does not mean a *person*, but an imparting spirit or principle, that "shall be in" a man, testifying of Christ and truth.

No person ever came as a comforter "to dwell," as Jesus had done, with the Apostles, or others, and openly and personally to testify of him; but it dwelt with them then; nor could a person "be in them." Remember, in these passages we have the declaration of the Saviour himself as to what is meant by the Holy Ghost, or Spirit. And he says further also that it "proceedeth from the Father." If it be said that there are passages which speak of God dwelling in you, and Christ dwelling in you, you dwelling in Christ; very well; but God and Christ have been shown and acknowledged to be persons, and so are you, and the figure of speech is therefore plainly understood. "If any man have not the Spirit of Christ, he is none of his." Rom. viii: 9. Now the Spirit of Christ here meant, is not the person of Christ; and it is the Spirit of God, and the Spirit of Christ that dwell, and not a person, in each case. In the instance of God dwelling, and Christ dwelling,

and you dwelling, the figure of speech is absolutely necessary; in the other, where the
Spirit is said to " dwell," or " be in you," the
figure is not necessary at all, because the word
used is naturally applicable to what proceeds
from a person, is the power of a person, or
the influence or impartation of a person. The
expressions " breath of the Almighty " and
" breath of the Lord," are used in the Bible
just as the expression " Spirit of God " is used.
" The Spirit of God hath made me, and the
breath of the Almighty hath given me life."
Job xxxii: 4. " By the word of the Lord were
the heavens made, and all the host of them
by the breath of his mouth." Psalm xxxiii:
6. We are not called upon to transfer personality to " breath " in these cases; and just
for the same reason that we are not compelled,
in fair argument, to say it is transferred to
spirit. St. Paul speaks of the spirit of a man
and the Spirit of God in the same sense, or in
a parallel sense: " For what man knoweth the

things of a man, save the spirit of a man which is in him? even so the things of God knoweth no man, but the Spirit of God." 1 Cor. ii: 11. By the spirit of a man, we do not understand his person; so by the Spirit of God, we are not to understand a person.

Let it not be said that notwithstanding our Lord does speak, as in the verses quoted from John, yet he uses the pronouns "he" and "him," and they indicate personality conclusively; such personification is very common in the Scriptures, and not uncommon in other writings, especially in oriental writings. The sun rejoiceth and knoweth his going down; the deep lifteth up his hands; wisdom crieth, &c. We might as well say, that, because the genius and decorum of the French language afford a feminine pronoun to the Czar, a remote age might fairly hold that it was conclusive evidence the word Czar meant a queen, and not an emperor.

In the second chapter of Acts, describing

the memorable day of Pentecost, the Scripture says "they were *all filled* with the Holy Ghost, and began to speak with other tongues, as the Spirit gave them utterance;" and in the thirty-third verse, St. Peter alludes to the promise of the Saviour, before quoted, and refers to the scene before them, as a fulfilment of the expected joy. Here is no *person* come; and surely it would be very absurd to say they were all filled with a person. Indeed, this was the enduement "with *power* from on high" promised to be sent *upon* them in the last chapter of Luke. "And behold, I send the promise of my Father upon you; but tarry ye in the city of Jerusalem, until ye be endued with power from on high." The "power" spoken of here is what is called the Comforter in St. John. This is plain. The expressions, "filled with the Holy Ghost," and "full of the Holy Ghost," are to be found frequently in the Evangelists, and in the -Acts; and "he shall baptize you with the

Holy Ghost," is also stated. We cannot imagine baptism with a person, although it is plain there is here a figure of speech; therefore, we think the purifying power or influence of God is meant. And the Apostles were so baptized at Pentecost. Acts i: 35. "And he breathed on them, and saith unto them, Receive ye the Holy Ghost." John xx: 22. "Have ye received the Holy Ghost since ye believed?" Acts xix: 2. "The Holy Ghost came on them." verse 6; "That they might receive the Holy Ghost." "And they *received* the Holy Ghost." Acts viii: 15–17. Our Lord said, "How much more shall your Heavenly Father *give* the Holy Spirit to them that ask him?" In Acts x: 38, St. Peter says: "How God *anointed* Jesus of Nazareth with the Holy Ghost and with *power*;" and in the 44, 45, and 47 verses it is said: "While Peter spake these words the Holy Ghost *fell* on all them which heard the word," and "on the Gentiles also was *poured out* the *gift* of the Holy Ghost,"

4

and "which have received the Holy Ghost."
St. Paul, in 8th Romans, speaks of the Spirit
of Him who raised up Jesus from the dead,
dwelling "in you," etc.   1 Cor. iii: 16. "The
Spirit of God dwelleth in you."

1 John iv: 3. "Hereby know ye the Spirit of
God. EVERY SPIRIT that witnesseth that Jesus
Christ is come in the flesh is of God."   In this
the Apostle surely means the influence that is
stirring in our hearts, that bears testimony of
Christ; and in the sixth verse he speaks of the
spirit of truth and the spirit of error, in the same
category, which excludes the idea of person.
And further, in this chapter he says: "Hereby know we that we dwell in him and he in
us, because he hath given us of his Spirit, and
we have seen and do *testify* that the Father
sent the Son to be the Saviour of the world."
Now, here is an impartation of the Spirit, or
a portion of it given us, and it is used in the
same sense as the spirit of truth, and as the
Comforter referred to by Jesus in the Evan-

gelists. In all these passages, (and others might be mentioned,) it seems to us, the Holy Spirit is spoken of so surely and distinctly, not as a person, but as a power, influence, or impartation, that we have sufficient explanation of the words when used in the 12th of Matthew, 3d of Mark, and 12th of Luke, before quoted.

As mentioned in 1st of Matthew and 1st of Luke, 35th verse, no man dare say that more was meant than the power of God.

If there are any stronger expressions in the Scriptures in favor of the doctrine of the personality of the Holy Spirit than those first referred to, we do not remember them. The 7th verse of the 5th chapter of 1 John is deemed spurious by biblical scholars, both Trinitarians and Unitarians. And we ask, where is the evidence to a rational mind, (that does not take things for granted because others say so,) of this personality, and of the person being, not the Father, but the same a the Father—one with him—a third person in a trinity? Is it in the nature of things? No. Is it to be found in the old Scriptures? No. Is it to be found in the belief of the Hebrew people, who received and kept these oracles? No.—And even the Shekinah of the tabernacle and the temple was but a presence and glory of God.—Is it to be found in the declarations of our Lord or his Apostles? No. Is the decree of the Council of Constantinople, enforced by acts of barbarous tyranny, sufficient to convince the intelligent inquirer of this age of enlightened; as it is of independent, thought? No. To such as hold to the infallibility of the Ecumenical Council, composed of whatever material it may have been, it is consistent, not only to hold this, but anything else it may have written down; but to us who rely on the Bible, and the common sense and mental advantages that God has given us, it is not sufficient, but opposed to the sources of truth.

But Unitarians do believe in the Holy Spirit

as imbuing our souls with good, testifying to our hearts of the Lord Jesus, saving us from our sins, and turning us to God our Father. The great truth of the presence, power, and influence of the Holy Spirit is to us of unutterable importance. It is a truth full of consolation and hope. It lies at the foundation of all spiritual religion. Without it religion would become mere formalism, and regeneration — that new birth, that spiritual renewal without which one cannot enter the kingdom of heaven — a meaningless term.

And we hold that His Holy Spirit is extended to every man, because God is impartial, and is the Father of every man; and we do not believe that a certain portion of his children are elected without any reference to good works, and that no others are redeemed by Christ — that "the rest of mankind God was pleased to pass by, and to ordain them to dishonor and wrath"—"fore-ordained to everlasting death." Westminster Con., chap. iii., sec. 3, 5, 6, 7. Such an impeachment of the Almighty Parent fills the soul with unutterable horror!

V. We are compelled to appeal to Scripture and reason from the creeds of men, on another subject. Christ is the Redeemer of the world. He came to call sinners to repentance; to reveal the true God as the Universal Father of love and mercy; to declare the enormity of sin; the forgiveness of God to them who repent and turn away from their transgressions; to save all men from sin and its consequences, by his sublime life and precepts; by his death and resurrection; and to bring "life and immortality to light through the gospel." He came not to work for us a salvation by appeasing the anger of God; but he came on a message of love — his whole life, his teachings, his example of obedience, humility, and piety, his reliance and whole trust in God; his sufferings, his death, and his resurrection, were an offering for us.

We are not saved by his death alone. Certainly the Scriptures do dwell upon his death with peculiar importance as a means of salvation; but it pleased God that we should have his teachings, and the instruction of his holy life also, as means to save us. "For if when we were enemies we were reconciled to God by the death of his Son; much more, being reconciled, we shall be *saved by his life.*" Rom. v: 10. His death and resurrection were the seals of his divine mission. His resurrection is dwelt upon by St. Peter and St. Paul as if necessary as his death. Without it preaching is vain, and faith is vain, and "ye are yet in your sins." 1 Cor. xv. chap. "It is Christ that died, *yea, rather, that is risen again*, who is even at the right hand of God, who also maketh intercession for us." Rom. viii: 4. "Was raised again for our justification." Rom. iv: 25. See 2, 10, 17, 26 chapters of Acts. "The like figure whereunto even baptism doth also now save us, (not the putting away the filth of the flesh, but the answer of a good conscience toward God,) by the resurrection of Jesus Christ." 1 Peter iii : 21.

The Saviour says : " I lay down my life, *that I might take it again.*" John x : 17. " It behoved Christ to suffer and to rise from the dead the third day, that *repentance and remission of sins should be preached in his name among all nations*, beginning at Jerusalem." Luke xxvi. chapter. Him hath God exalted to be a Prince and a Saviour, to give *repentance* to Israel and *forgiveness of sins.*" Acts v : 31.

But his death was necessary on account of our sins. And when we contemplate his sufferings, brought about by our transgressions, O, what can so powerfully impress us with the awfulness of sin!

The creeds of men represent the Deity as angry for a violation of his law, and demanding satisfaction for the violation, so that the *law* might be upheld. They teach that God would not, or could not, pardon, according to his government, without a satisfaction; that

Christ was "crucified, dead, and buried, to reconcile his Father to us, and to be a sacrifice, not only for original guilt, but also, for actual sins of men." 2 Art. Church of England. The Westminster Confession says, that by the sacrifice of himself, etc., he "hath fully satisfied the justice of his Father, and purchased not only reconciliation," etc.*

Unitarians hold that, according to the Scriptures, our Heavenly Father was always placable; was always ready, willing, and able, without violation of his law, to forgive us our sins, on repentance and turning to him. That no satisfaction was ever demanded, or could have been made. What is meant by satisfaction to *God* for the sins of men? Are not these words without meaning? God was always merciful as now. "His mercy endureth forever." If

---

* We wonder if those who hold that Christ was God, the same as the Father, do not see the inconsistency of his having made a satisfaction to himself. Even little children can see this is a contradiction. The same person cannot be payor and payee. It is useless to say this satisfaction by one person to the same one person, is a mystery. It is no mystery, but a naked contradiction.

there is anything that we are sure is stated
in the Bible, it is the absolute law of God
declared in that book, that "if the wicked
will turn from all his sins that he hath committed, and keep all my statutes, and do that
which is lawful and right, he shall surely live,
he shall not die." Ezek. xviii. "Let the
wicked forsake his way and the unrighteous
man his thoughts, and let him return unto the
Lord, and he will have mercy upon him; and
to our God, for he will abundantly pardon."
Isa. lv: 7. "For thou desirest not sacrifice;
else would I give it; thou delightest not in
burnt offering. The sacrifices of God are a
broken spirit; a broken and contrite heart, O
God, thou wilt not despise." Ps. li: 16, 17.
Repentance and remissions of sins was, as it
is now, the law of the unchangeable God. No
sacrifice of the Old Testament was made *to
procure* pardon in itself, unless it were only of
a ritual offense. An oblation could not change
God. It could not make any compensation,

or any benefit to him, or, in any possible sense, be of any value to him. It was of value to, and operated on, the party who made the sacrifice. It reminded him, (and others,) of the wickedness of transgression, of the necessity of obedience, and of the forgiving power and mercy of God. Let us not mistake the meaning of sacrifice; surely no one can believe that the smoke of incense of the old ceremonial could, in itself, affect the God of Heaven. "In burnt offerings, and sacrifices for sin thou hast had no pleasure." Heb. x: 6. God was not reconciled to men by the oblation of the altar, but men were reconciled to God by returning to him; and they found pardon of sin in his inflexible law, when they did return.

There is no such statement in the New Testament *as that God was reconciled to man* by the death of Christ; or *that Christ satisfied* the justice of his Father, and purchased reconciliation. God loved and pitied the sinner, "like as a father pitieth his children;" he demanded nothing to reconcile him; he asked no satisfaction of an innocent being for the guilty. This "satisfaction" is a crude notion of such men as believed that God was such a being as made and appointed some men absolutely to eternal damnation; it is part of what they called a "plan of salvation." It is a plan, but of their own invention—they had no word of God for it. They put man's vindiction, and selfish, stubborn exaction into the heart of that Infinite Parent, who bends over us in a father's mercy and care!

How could that satisfy that God who "*Is Love?*" His law was not like our law, founded on policy,* and demanding a penalty to satisfy and uphold its authority, and to deter those who see the guilty punished. We cannot see

---

* By "policy" we do not mean mere expediency. Law has a broader basis. But we mean to refer to that NECESSITY of looking to the end aimed at, which binds all governments of men. God's law is a perfect rule to every individual man, under all circumstances—a system of Omniscient uprightness.

when men do repent in their hearts. He can. Our law must deter by punishment; and it withholds forgiveness, even when assured of repentance. He has no such necessity, no such law. His mercy and his justice are the same; and when men separate them, they detract from God, and compare Him to themselves. Our justice, founded on policy, must be separate from mercy. But *we* would not exact, as a satisfaction, the punishment of the innocent, to purchase mercy for the guilty. "Shall mortal man be more just than God? Shall a man be more just than his Maker?"

We reject the doctrine that God was reconciled to us, or that a satisfaction was made. These impeach the love and mercy of our Father in Heaven. Our Lord's words are plain: "For God so loved the world, that he gave his only begotten Son, that whosoever believeth on him, should not perish, but have everlasting life. For God sent not his Son into the world to condemn the world, but that the world through

him might be saved." John iii: 16, 17. The
Scripture says, we were reconciled to God. Rom.
v: 10.* "And all things are of God, who hath
reconciled us to himself by Jesus Christ, and
hath given us the ministry of reconciliation, to
wit: that God was in Christ reconciling the
world unto himself, not imputing their trespass-
es unto them; and hath committed unto us the
word of reconciliation. Now, then, we are am-
bassadors for Christ, as though God did beseech
you by us: we pray you in Christ's stead, be
ye reconciled to God. For he hath made him
to be sin for us, who knew no sin; *that we might
be made the righteousness of God in him.*" 2 Cor.
v. 18–21. Not to satisfy or reconcile God,
but that we by his gospel, sealed by his death,
might be made righteous in repentance and
following him.

---

* The word atonement only occurs once in the common English
translation of the New Testament. The original word means reconciliation, and it is so translated in every other place. And
where the word is rendered atonement, it is said: "We have now
received the atonement"—not that it had affected God. Rom. v: 11

We reject the doctrine that Adam's transgression was imputed to us, and we were guilty of it. This is nowhere found in the Scriptures; it is unreasonable; it is impossible; and it impeaches the justice of God. It would make God a tyrant, and not a merciful Father. *The artificial notion that we could sin by another, before we had an existence, is merely absurd.* God made us as we are—imperfect and liable to sin. As our Maker, he loved us, and made it *our law* to repent of this sin and forsake it; and he made it *His law*, that, on repentance and returning to him, he would forgive. He never said he wanted any other reconciliation to us but this. He has told us "He is faithful and just to forgive us our sins."

But the creeds tell us, that by man's corrupt nature, inherited from Adam, "he is utterly indisposed, disabled, and made opposite unto all that is spiritually good, and wholly inclined to all evil, and that continually;" and that "the fall brought upon mankind the loss

of communion with God, his displeasure, and
curse; so as we are *by nature children of wrath,*
bond slaves to Satan, and *justly liable* to all
punishment in this world, and that which
is to come." Westm. The Church of England, in the 9th Art., after reciting the fall
and depravity of mankind, says: "And therefore, in every person born into this world, it
deserveth God's wrath and denunciation."
What awful imputations on "the Father of
Mercies," on "the God of Love!" Now, Unitarians do not believe that God has made man
without any good in him, wholly inclined to
all evil; they do not believe that he comes
into the world liable to any punishment, as he
has committed no sin; but that he is the subject of God's merciful care. He is capable
from his nature of obedience by God's grace;
else to address the commandments to him
would be vain; and to punish him for diso-
bedience would be unjust. To make a being
with a nature wholly inclined to evil, and

when he commits evil, (which of course he must do, with such a nature,) to demand a satisfaction, over and beyond his sincere repentance and forsaking of sin, is to do what would certainly not consist with our notions of man's mercy;—how shall we permit any thing written by men, to make us ascribe such to the mercy of the MOST HIGH?

Unitarians believe that salvation by our Lord's mission is in all things of God's love to his sinful creatures; that Christ was not a substitution for us to bear the wrath of God; that our sins were not imputed to him; that no satisfaction was demanded, and none was made. Some of them believe, whatever is said of sacrifice in reference to the death of Christ, is merely figurative, so far as the similitude to the Jewish oblations is indicated; while others, (among whom is the writer of this report,) believe that there was a real expiation, in love to us; not to affect God, but in His wise and incomprehensible Providence, to accomplish our salvation.

5

VI. As to the miracles of the New Testament; either they are true, and are exceptions to the laws of nature, as we generally understand them, or the record made of them is merely false. There is no middle ground for our philosophy. It is apparent to every reader, whose mind has not been fixed by reasonings, too keen and refined to be understood by plain sense, that it was the intention of the narrators to give these instances we call miracles, as evidence of the Saviour's Divine Power. According to the account in the gospel, Jesus said to John's disciples, who made the memorable inquiry of him, "The blind receive their sight, and the lame walk, the lepers are cleansed, and the deaf hear, *the dead are raised up*, and the poor have the gospel preached to them." These facts were given to John as *evidence* that he was the Messiah. The great miracle of the resurrection of our Lord himself, is so distinctly stated in the gospels, and so dwelt upon by the Apostles, that any argument, however ingenious, to attempt to support the fact as *apparent* but *not real*, is merely offensive to honest downrightness and common sense; and imputes to the New Testament indirection that is nothing less than the holding forth of what is not true.

Certainly we deem the holy morality, the piety of the gospel — too high for earth — convincing evidence of its divine origin; but the Scriptures have not left to men of all conditions, this moral testimony alone, — conclusive only to the most enlightened minds, — but have subjoined tangible facts for the assistance of our weak and fallible natures — mercifully for us who do not always feel the elevation of obedience to God.

We have thus stated some of the reasons why we reject the additions made to the Christian faith by a temporal authority, or that which undertook to govern men, not in the meekness of its Great Author, but by the strength of coarseness and assumption — the domination of semi-barbarous bishops, and semi-barbarous princes.

The history of the times when these things were done, "is like the streets of a great city on the day of a military or ecclesiastical procession, when all laymen, or civilians, are ordered to keep out of the way." Nobody was allowed to have any opinion but the bishops and the emperor; and the bishops themselves must have the opinion of the emperor, or leave their diocese; in other language, go into exile on his decree. *At no Ecumenical Council did they make any articles of faith for the people, but what the emperor approved.* At Nice the Emperor Constantine was present from day to day, and wrote a part of the creed himself, according to Eusebius. This emperor pretended to have renounced paganism; but he was not baptized and admitted into the church for years afterwards; and the same year in which he called this first Ecumenical Council, he, who had caused his father-in-law to be put to death, murdered his son Crispus, and murdered his nephew Licinius. Such was the man whose authority is exerted on the faith of the followers of the meek, the pure, and holy Saviour of sinners.

And so the same clamping down of power on free inquiry and free judgment, was practiced in a later day, in making of the Westminster Confession and Catechism; for the Parliament appointed every man to the Assembly, by name, and confined, by the ordinance that called them, their consideration to "such matters and things" as should "be proposed unto them by both or either of the said Houses of Parliament, and *no other*;" and what they did was to be merely advisory, to be approved or rejected by the Parliament; and it was so approved in 1649. Now, is it possible that we can take such things as all these, as chief sources of religious truth, unless our own researches can find them upheld by the Bible?

Can we give up our own judgments to men of such times? As we are responsible to God for the "search of the Scriptures," we cannot.

It may be asked, How is it that the decrees made at Nice, at Constantinople, and at Chalcedon, which made up the doctrine of the Trinity, etc., should have had the reliance of a majority of those professing the Christian faith for so long a time? It is not difficult to see how this has been—every clear judgment of human nature can discern it as a natural result. The decrees made were enforced by the political as well as by the spiritual authority, by the anathemas of the bishops, and the edicts of a tyrant demanding men to yield conscience and reason, or be destroyed. And the world not long afterwards, passed into the hands of barbarians, and dark ages ensued — darker than when the mitre and crown began to *make reason and religion for a man*—and when it awoke again, the habits of ancestry, the faith of parents, were on the children. — Had the decrees set up other doctrines, would not these doctrines have had the same force, the same veneration, to-day, as what they did set up? *Who can deny this?* Nothing is so strong to bind men as the religion of their ancestors. Even superstition is entailed, and wears not out with ages. The subject of religious faith is an awful subject. We are afraid even to question a creed that we have been taught is nothing less than our salvation. If men have been taught, by inherited instruction, in the church, and at the fireside, such a doctrine for instance, as that Christ was really God, they feel as if they were impeaching holiness, and doing blasphemy to doubt it. And to pause about what we have heard in the prayers of our fathers and mothers, seems almost like disrespect; and it requires heroism to *search* if it be true.—The sentiment is beautiful, sublime; but truth is first and above all.— Thus succeeding generations are induced to yield the implicit reliance, which belongs only to the scriptures of truth, to that which was made by usurped authority, enforced by oppression and wrong.

It takes strength to unfetter the reason, and to strike for truth only; but this is an age of moral courage, self-reliance, and love of truth. God loves the man that loves the truth; God loves a brave man, and a man who is brave enough to come through ranks and throngs of bishops, emperors, kings, and parliaments, to inquire OF HIM for truth.

VII. We wish to see the religion of Jesus Christ pure, plain, simple, sublime, as it came from our Lord and his Apostles—relieved from entanglements of human invention or superstition. The precepts of Christ can be understood by the most uneducated and artless mind. What is necessary to enable us to be partakers of his salvation, is to be comprehended by the meanest capacity. But these truths overlaid by subtle dogmas that no mind can contain, that no effort can reconcile, make that more than a mystery, worse than confounded, which was the end to which the Saviour was born and came into the world. He came "to bear witness to the truth." To these things, we insist, he never did bear witness.

How beautiful and how majestic would religion look, robed again in the untouched white of the sermon on the mount!

And let us remember, that whatever we may say or dispute about the doctrines of the church, this is the great truth: That piety to God is the duty and the great end of life; that without an humble reliance on our Heavenly Father, and obedience to his commandments by a holy life, all doctrines of a metaphysical or of a Scriptural faith, are nothing to bring us to salvation.

Your Committee recommend to the Conference the doctrines contained in the Resolution,

and in this Report. All of which is respectfully submitted.

HENRY PIRTLE.
WM. G. ELIOT.
JOHN H. HEYWOOD.

13th May, 1854.

REPORT ON

SUNDAY SCHOOLS,

PRESENTED BY

REV. WM. A. FULLER,

OF QUINCY, ILLINOIS.

REPORT.

The subject which is to be brought before you in this Report, may not appear to be of so much immediate importance as some others; but we may, with confidence, presume that it is of sufficient importance to claim the consideration of the Conference.

The question, what can and ought to be done to promote the interests and efficiency of our Sunday Schools, as a means for imparting right religious influences and instructions to the young, lies upon the border of a very important theme, which, (though it comes not within the sphere of our report,) gives color and shape to what we propose to offer. We allude, of course, to Christian nurture, training, and education in general; and in particular, to the sphere and sovereignty of church influence and authority over its consecrated lambs.

What is it, and what its extent, and how ought it to be exerted?

Whatever view may be held upon this subject, and whatever answer be given to these interrogations, we are convinced of nothing so much as its importance to the interests of the Redeemer's kingdom, and as a great and thrilling question of duty. Has it any especial bearing upon our Sunday Schools? We believe it has, and perhaps we may in some degree bring out our meaning by an immediate application.

Concerning the condition of our Sunday Schools, their members, and the number of children in average attendance in proportion to our several congregations and churches; and concerning the methods of procedure, and use made of them, as religious schools, your committee cannot definitely speak. Some effort was made to obtain these items of interest, but failing in the attempt, it was dropped. Yet we presume that what from observation and experience we know, may be taken as a guide to what lies beyond the limits of our knowledge. And presuming thus, we ask your attention particularly to what appears to our mind to be of considerable, nay, of unusual importance — to the simple fact, that the Sunday School is the only medium through which our churches can immediately reach the young, and impart direct religious instruction to them, aside from ordinary services. This statement may require modifying, perhaps, but in the main it is true; and does not a question here present itself worthy of serious meditation, because of sacred and thrilling import;—whether, with the views we hold of the primal innocence of the soul, as it comes from God, and of its susceptibility of being moulded into the divine likeness of Christ, more and more perfectly, through right religious nurture and education, sustained by the sanctions and authority of the church; purging, by a progressive life, the natural man of inherited tendencies to evil; and fostering a divine growth, so that babes shall be Christian babes, then Christian youth, and Christians in maturity;—whether with these views, which at once reveal a sacred trust of duty to the church as well as the home, the practice of our churches is altogether consistent as a general thing?

Be this as it may, we present the statement simply which we have made. We have departed, and churches of other denominations have departed, in this from the beaten track of our fathers, and perhaps for the better; still we believe it ought to be the object of the church of Christ to "bring the young,"—upon whom the moral hope of the world, as well as that of our churches themselves, depends— "to Christ," by all the sanctions of her authority and influence; and that in the absence of other means—if indeed other means, and better adapted to the end, could be found—the sanctions of her authority ought to be given, and the strength of her influence ought to be made to rest upon and be felt in the Sunday School, as her fitting nursery; and that this obligation rests with peculiar weight upon ourselves, as it is certain that our peculiar sphere is more emphatically that of growth than conquest.

We discard the false issues and unjustifiable proceedings of modern revivalism. What then remains for us but to forestall its necessity by better methods and a more living way, if we should shun the sad result of building up churches with little or no other religious life in them, than such as may be too justly characterized in the words of Sidney Smith, as a " decent debility." And though it may be our great endeavor to turn men from sin to holiness, and lead them to the reconciling grace of God in Christ, we must look to the young for the formation of right religious characters —for that reformation in progress and growth which is the hope of the church and the world and which shall be permanent and life-givin as the reign of Christ on earth.

The term Sunday School, (for these and other reasons,) does not truly represent the fitting character of these nurseries of the church and of religious life in the church.

It was applied to an institution originally intrinsically different in character — an institution established for the purpose of imparting ordinary instruction to pauper children. It does not import that devotional element, or represent that directness and concentration of holy influence which should characterize and pervade these Schools. But though our children in general are not in need, as were those for whom Sunday Schools were originally established, of ordinary instructions in secular knowledge, the system as a means of imparting religious instruction, has by unanimous consent been adopted. And well that it is so, as every other direct connection with them, and hold upon them, on the part of the church, seems to have been parted with, or absorbed *into this.*

Therefore, to approach particularly the object before us, your Committee earnestly recommend, that the Conference take the interests of these Sunday Religious Schools under its fostering care; that there be matured and presented to our churches, such suggestions as shall truly embody and represent the importance of the subject, and such recommendations as shall best promote their efficiency as a means of grace to the "little ones" of the household of faith, and ultimately to our children's children. We ask that the Conference set its seal upon them definitely, as the nurseries of those elements and principles which stamps them with a positively religious character and aspect, with reference to the formation and development of religious faith and affections in the young.

Furthermore, believing that this is what we should aim to accomplish, your Committee suggest, First, As requisite and necessary, in order to give our Sunday Schools the efficiency which they ought to have; that pastors beand become — if indeed they are not — pastors in an especial manner, of this branch of the church, aiming to bring under their watchful care and vigilant control all its interests and exercises. Second, That children be taught in these schools, and elsewhere, and impressed with the conviction that they are of the kingdom of heaven and church of Christ, not born out of it, but into it; to grow up in the loving nurture and fearing admonition of the Lord. Third, Also, that teachers be persons of religious character and experience, who, by their indwelling faith and devout frame of mind, are rendered capable of imparting to the young the bread of Life. And lastly, to secure this more fully and effectually, that more strictly religious and devotional exercises are desirable and necessary.

Your Committee, in regard to this last suggestion, can only say, after some experience, during which they have had the charge of the exercises of this branch of the church, that its importance has been fully demonstrated, as interesting the young, for there is no part of the exercises with which they enter with more willing heartiness — as developing in them, legitimately and properly, devotional feelings, giving them a religious bias, and helping them to realize that they are participants in public religious worship.

The order of exercises adopted has been more in the form of worship than otherwise. The exercises have been more those of a religious assembly than as, in any sense, a school. This has been the order: an introductory exhortation or address, reading and responses, prayers in which all unite; then prayer individually offered in behalf of children and teachers; after which are hymns, instructions, and benediction.

What appears to be needed for immediate and general use, is a manual of devotion, embodying substantially this form, or something like it, adapted to children, with hymns and appropriate tunes set to them.

The form generally indicated is our own. The hymns we have used are of another denomination, which, in some respects, are exceptionable. We have not been able to procure a book of this sort, nor do we know of any in existence; certainly none such as in every respect—or even in most respects—meets our idea of what one should be. We therefore respectfully suggest, First, That the Conference procure a work of this sort, for general use; and if not otherwise to be obtained, that a committee be appointed to prepare one. Second, That the series of works embodying a systematic course of instruction, recently edited and published in Boston, be procured and recommended to our churches. And Third, That hereafter the statistics of our Sunday Religious Schools, together with all other matters of interest appertaining to them, be annually reported; as a source of general interest;

as a stimulus to healthy improvement; and that due consideration may be given to the subject. All of which is respectfully submitted by your Committee.

Lightning Source UK Ltd.
Milton Keynes UK
UKHW050650111118
331957UK00027B/273/P